SMALLER HOUSES
OF THE 1920s

55 Examples

ETHEL B. POWER

DOVER PUBLICATIONS, INC.
Mineola, New York

Bibliographical Note

This Dover edition, first published in 2007, is an unabridged republication of *The Smaller American House: Fifty-five Houses of the Less Expensive Type Selected from the Recent Work of Architects in all Parts of the Country,* published by Little, Brown, and Company, Boston, 1927.

Library of Congress Cataloging-in-Publication Data

Power, Ethel B.
   Smaller houses of the 1920s : 55 examples / Ethel B. Power.
      p. cm.
   Originally published: Boston : Little, Brown, and Co., 1927.
   ISBN 13: 978-0-486-46049-9
   ISBN 10: 0-486-46049-5
1. Small houses—United States—Designs and plans. 2. Architecture—United States—20th century—Designs and plans. I. Title.
   NA7208.P69 2007
   728'.370973—dc22

                                                           2007003354

Manufactured in the United States of America
Dover Publications, Inc., 31 East 2nd Street, Mineola, New York 11501

FOREWORD

STUDYING plans is to almost all grown-ups as enjoyable a game as is playing
house to children. We like to consider each new plan that we become
acquainted with, which at all approaches a solution of our problem, as a
setting for ourselves, our family, and our possessions, and to cross its imaginary threshold, fold its imaginary walls around us, and make believe
we are its fortunate inhabitants, even as do children in their hastily
improvised tents. We like to live ourselves into each corner, chamber, and
closet, and play at keeping house there, until we discover the virtues and
defects of this temporarily adopted playhouse, and then, when we prove it
inadequate, abandon it, as indifferently as does a lobster its shell.

The purpose of this book is, first of all, to give you a number of plans
for playing just such a game, showing with them the walls that the architect
has erected according to the wishes and requirements of his client. Your
wishes and requirements may modify these walls, even as they will the
plans, adding a doorway here, changing a material there, increasing breadth
or width until you have, in the end, a concept of a house which, it is to be
hoped, will some day become the outward expression of the results of this
mental exploration.

The compelling motive, therefore, that prompted this publication was
the desire to show the best of the smaller houses that have been built re-
cently in this country in order that you may build your castle upon a worthy
foundation. The houses selected were not chosen to demonstrate any theory
of the desirability of one style over another, or of a supposed superiority of
any one material over another, or to emphasize any locality. If one style or
one material predominates, or if one section of the country is more fully
represented than another, that is by pure chance. Nor were these houses
selected with any idea of illustrating, by including examples of all types, the
recent development of the small house in this country; although the relation
of contemporary American house architecture to established European
styles, and the extent to which it has broken away from precedent and
contributed to the creation of an independent American style, make a
tempting subject which many of the houses shown would very well illustrate.

That these houses do run the gamut of styles, from those with their roots
in European precedents to those of recent graftings, is due to the fact that
as much variety as possible was sought. Actually, they represent, it is
believed, a typical cross section of present-day domestic architecture, and
one cut on a high plane of merit. To find this plane was not difficult, for

small-house architecture in America to-day, it is generally conceded, has reached a greater degree of excellence than has contemporary small-house architecture elsewhere. In saying this, however, we must not forget to acknowledge our debt to those European countries which have contributed the corner stones of its foundation.

For those who are interested to trace this debt, it may be plainly perceived in many of the houses included here. The house of Miss Emery, for instance, bears a close resemblance to the early New England farmhouse that was, in turn, highly reminiscent of the mediæval cottage with second-story over-hang, small diamond-paned windows, and long, sloping roof line, with which the Colonists had been familiar in the mother country; and the house of Mr. Keffer has many of the elements of the Normandy cottage. The house of Mrs. Mowery, on the other hand, and the house in Chestnut Hill by Gordon Allen, show less distinctly their antecedents, and seem more indigenous products. They are primarily logical expressions of their plans, which are highly individualized and obvious solutions of circumscribed conditions. Indeed, perhaps one of the most striking features of all these houses is the extreme variety of their plans; the many ways that the very limited number of given units have been combined, without sacrifice of convenience or economy, into a workable whole. And it is perhaps in the plans of our small houses that American architects first demonstrated their ingenuity and originality, stimulated by the exigencies of economy and a growing sense on the part of the housewife of the necessity for applying to the business of house-keeping the principles of efficiency that obtained in the masculine world.

The form of the book, that of a series of illustrations without text, was chosen because it was thought that the houses speak for themselves, and that they would tell their story better if the maximum amount of space possible were devoted to the half-tones. The captions make no attempt to appraise the house described. They merely add those facts that the camera could not portray, but which seem necessary in order to complete the picture. The houses are grouped according to the simple classification of materials in the following order: wood, stucco, concrete, brick, and stone.

ETHEL B. POWER

BOSTON, MASSACHUSETTS
January 10, 1927

ARCHITECTS REPRESENTED

OWNERS OF HOUSES SHOWN

Smaller Houses of the 1920s

55 Examples

THE HALL IN THE MOWERY HOUSE, OPENING DIRECTLY INTO THE LIVING ROOM TWO STEPS BELOW IT, HAS A FLOOR
OF BLACK AND WHITE MARBLE TILES

THE HOUSE OF MRS. ELDRED MOWERY

Eldred Mowery, Architect

THE HOUSE IS BUILT ON A SLOPING LOT, STEEP ENOUGH TO ALLOW A GARAGE UNDER THE PORCH, IN AN
OLD APPLE ORCHARD IN DEDHAM, MASSACHUSETTS. THE WALLS ARE OF HAND-SPLIT CYPRESS SHINGLES
STAINED WHITE, THE ROOF IS OF CEDAR SHINGLES WEATHERED, AND THE SHUTTERS ARE PAINTED BLUE-GREEN

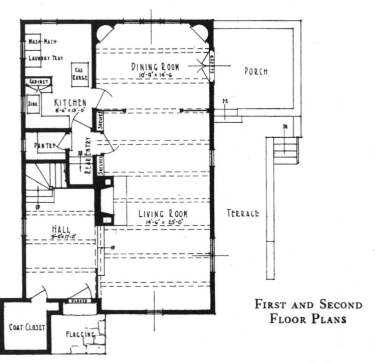

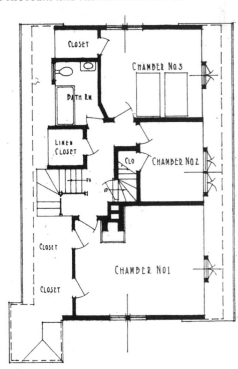

FIRST AND SECOND
FLOOR PLANS

IN THE LIVING ROOM OF THE MOWERY HOUSE THE WOODWORK IS COUNTRY PINE, STAINED A WASP'S-NEST GRAY THROUGH WHICH THE NATURAL WARM TONES OF THE WOOD SHOW, GIVING IT A WEATHERED APPEARANCE. THE WALLS ARE FINISHED WITH A TROWEL COAT OF WOOD-FIBRE PLASTER, COLORED WITH YELLOW OCHRE TO A SOFT BEIGE TONE

IN THE DINING ROOM OF THE SAME HOUSE THE WOODWORK IS PAINTED WHITE, AND THE WALLS ARE COVERED WITH PAPER HAVING A SOFT GRAY BACKGROUND, WITH TINY BOUQUETS OF BRIGHT ROSES IN SMALL MEDALLIONS WHICH VIE IN GAYNESS WITH THE WINDOW SHADES OF CHINTZ. THE TABLE IS AN OLD KITCHEN ONE OF CURLY MAPLE AND THE HITCHCOCK CHAIRS ARE PAINTED YELLOW

A House in Larchmont, New York

Walker & Gillette, Architects

A COLONIAL COTTAGE 25′ X 40′ OVER ALL, FACING SOUTH. IT HAS WALLS OF STRAW-
COLORED SHINGLES LAID 12″ TO 14″ TO THE WEATHER, WITH PINE TRIM PAINTED
CREAM COLOR AND BLINDS A DULL BLUE. THE ROOF IS OF GRAY SHINGLES. IN THE
LIVING ROOM THE 3 X 6 FLOOR BEAMS OF THE ROOM ABOVE ARE EXPOSED

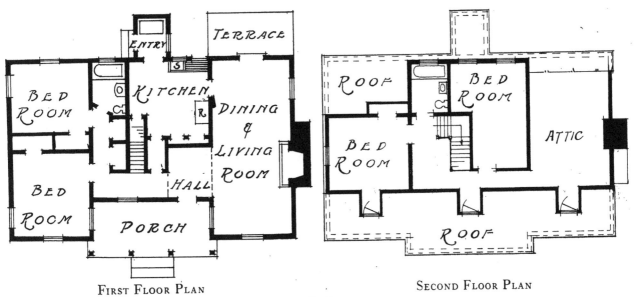

FIRST FLOOR PLAN · SECOND FLOOR PLAN

The House of Miss Georgia Emery

Henry Atherton Frost & Charles W. Killam, Associated Architects

A COLONIAL HOUSE IN THE MANNER OF THE SEVENTEENTH CENTURY, LOCATED AT THE
FOOT OF MT. MONADNOCK IN NEW HAMPSHIRE. ITS WALLS ARE OF PINE CLAPBOARDS
STAINED AND WEATHERED, WITH TRIM OF CYPRESS AND PINE TREATED SIMILARLY.
THE DOOR IS PAINTED GREEN AND THE SHUTTERS ARE STAINED TO MATCH THE HOUSE.
THE ROOF HAS NATURAL WEATHERED CEDAR SHINGLES

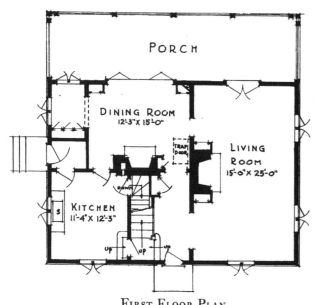

FIRST FLOOR PLAN

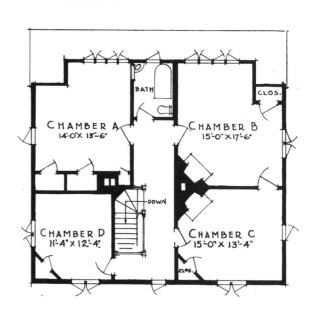

SECOND FLOOR PLAN

THE WOODWORK IN THE DINING ROOM, INCLUD-
ING THE CORNER CUPBOARD, IS PAINTED A
CREAM COLOR

THE WOODWORK IN THE HALL IS NATURAL
CYPRESS, OILED, AND THE FLOOR IS OF HAND-
MADE RED QUARRY TILE

FLOWERS GROW LUXURIANTLY IN A SMALL ENCLOSED DOORYARD GARDEN

IN THE UPPER HALL OF THE EMERY HOUSE THE JACOBEAN STAIRWAY IS AN ATTRACTIVE FEATURE, AND THE FURNITURE HERE AS ELSEWHERE IS IN CHARACTER WITH THE MEDIÆVAL STYLE OF THE HOUSE. THE WALLS ARE OF TANCOLORED PLASTER, AND HERE, AS THROUGHOUT THE HOUSE, ARE HUNG PIECES OF OLD FRENCH AND ENGLISH, COTTON PRINTS, SIMPLY FRAMED

THE HOUSE OF ROBERT W. ESTABROOK, ESQ.

Stanley B. Parker, Architect

THIS HOUSE OF WOOD-FRAME AND MASONRY CONSTRUCTION IS IN WABAN,
MASSACHUSETTS. THE FRONT IS OF NARROW CLAPBOARDS PAINTED WHITE,
WHILE THE ENDS ARE OF BRICK, ESPECIALLY PLEASING IN COLOR, AND LAID
IN ALTERNATE ROWS OF STRETCHERS AND HEADERS. THE SHUTTERS AND
DOOR ARE A BRIGHT GREEN, AND THE ROOF IS OF SLATE

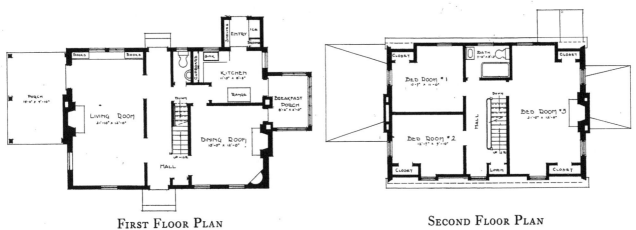

FIRST FLOOR PLAN   SECOND FLOOR PLAN

THE HOUSE OF DR. FRANCIS COLLINS

Dwight James Baum, Architect

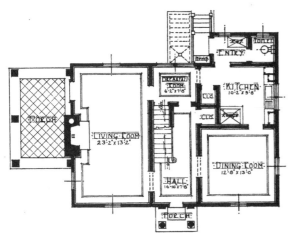

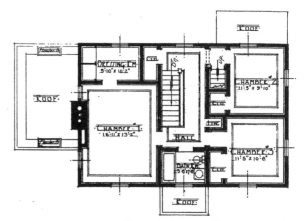

FIRST FLOOR PLAN   SECOND FLOOR PLAN

A HOUSE OF EARLY GREEK-REVIVAL TYPE, BUILT IN FIELDSTON, NEW YORK. THE
EXTERIOR WALLS ARE OF PINE, WITH ENDS OF WIDE CLAPBOARDS AND FRONT OF SHIP-
LAP. THE HOUSE IS PAINTED WHITE AND HAS A WHITE DOOR AND BLINDS OF DARK
GREEN AND ROOF OF SHINGLES, ALSO GREEN. THIS HOUSE HAS A SQUARE, COM-
PACT PLAN AND A SIMPLE ELEVATION, ATTAINING DISTINCTION BY ITS CAREFULLY
STUDIED DETAIL

THE DOORWAY HAS CLASSIC MOULDINGS, CAREFULLY ADJUSTED TO THE SCALE OF THE MATERIAL OF WHICH THEY
ARE MADE

A Cottage in Glen Cove, New York

Charles S. Keefe, Architect

THE WALLS OF THIS HOUSE ARE COVERED ON THE OUTSIDE WITH HAND-SPLIT CYPRESS SHINGLES LAID 11″ TO THE WEATHER AND PAINTED WHITE. INSIDE THEY ARE OF BUFF-COLORED PLASTER ON METAL LATH. THE EXTERIOR TRIM IS OF WHITE PINE, ALSO PAINTED WHITE. THE BLINDS ARE DARK GREEN AND THE ROOF OF GRAY SHINGLES

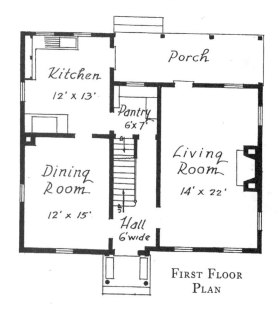

FIRST FLOOR
PLAN

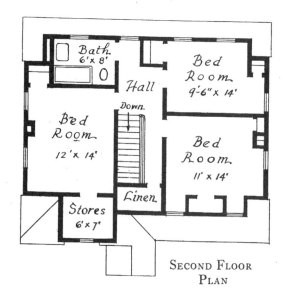

SECOND FLOOR
PLAN

THE HOUSE OF MISS ELIZABETH McJ. TYNG

Charles S. Keefe, Architect

TERRACE

OWN ROOM
12'-0" x 15'-0"

SUN PORCH
10'-0" x 15'-6"

KITCHEN
9'-6" x 10'-0"

LIVING ROOM
13'-0" x 20'-0"

GUEST RM
11'-6" x 13'-0"

HALL

FIRST FLOOR
PLAN

THIS HOUSE IN PALO ALTO, CALIFORNIA, HAS WALLS OF WIDE SIDING OF REDWOOD PAINTED WHITE, AND GREEN BLINDS. THE ROOF IS OF SHINGLES LEFT TO WEATHER. THE OUTSIDE TRIM IS OF REDWOOD, WHILE THE WOODWORK INSIDE IS OF PINE, PAINTED WHITE THROUGHOUT

THE DETAIL OF THIS HOUSE BEARS A CLOSE RESEMBLANCE TO THAT OF THE COTTAGE IN GLEN COVE ON THE PRECEDING PAGE, BECAUSE THE OWNER HAD SEEN THE LATTER AND WISHED A HOUSE OF SIMILAR TYPE, ADAPTED TO HER PARTICULAR NEEDS. THE FLOOR PLANS ARE ENTIRELY DISSIMILAR

The House of Sheffield A. Arnold, Esq.

Mowll & Rand, Architects

AN EXCELLENT ADAPTATION OF THE EARLY AMERICAN TYPE OF HOUSE, WITH SLIGHT
OVERHANG AND CARVED DROPS. THE EXTERIOR WALLS ARE OF SHINGLES STAINED
WHITE; THE SHUTTERS ARE GREEN; THE ROOF IS OF GRAY SHINGLES. THE CHIMNEY IS
OF BRICK, PAINTED WHITE WITH A BLACK CAP. THE HOUSE, IN WABAN, MASSACHU-
SETTS, IS SITUATED ON A CORNER LOT EXCEPTIONALLY WELL PLANTED BY ITS OWNER,
WHO IS A LANDSCAPE ARCHITECT

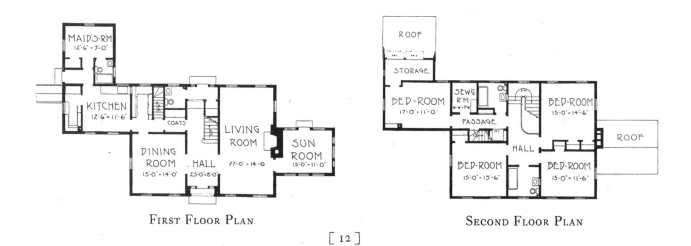

FIRST FLOOR PLAN   SECOND FLOOR PLAN

A WELL HOUSE COMPOSES ATTRACTIVELY WITH BOTH THE SUN ROOM AND REAR ELL

AT THE BACK OF THE HOUSE IS A GRASS TERRACE WITH PERENNIAL BORDERS

THE HOUSE OF MRS. HELEN T. B. CROCKER

Prentice Sanger, Architect

THIS COTTAGE IS BUILT ON A STEEPLY SLOPING LOT IN FITCHBURG, MASSACHUSETTS.
ITS WALLS ARE OF WIDE SIDING AND MATCHED BOARDS, PAINTED A CREAM COLOR; THE
SHUTTERS ARE NATURAL WOOD, OILED, AND THE ROOF IS OF UNFADING SLATE IN BLUES,
GREENS, AND YELLOWS. THE HOUSE IS FACED SO THAT ONLY THE DINING ROOM IS ON
THE STREET SIDE, AND THE LIVING ROOM AND VERANDAH HAVE THE IMPORTANT VIEW

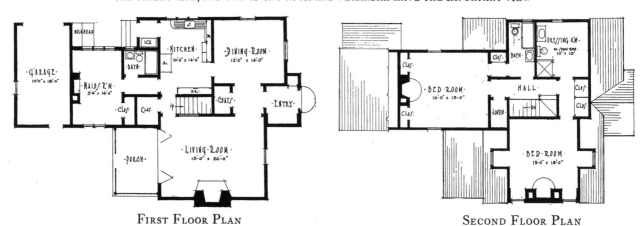

FIRST FLOOR PLAN   SECOND FLOOR PLAN

THE HOUSE OF ARTHUR L. WILLIS, ESQ.

Roger H. Bullard, Architect

THIS EXCELLENT INTERPRETATION OF AN EARLY NEW ENGLAND GAMBREL-ROOF
COTTAGE IS IN FLUSHING, LONG ISLAND. IT IS OF WOOD-FRAME CONSTRUCTION, WITH
WALLS OF NARROW CEDAR SIDING PAINTED WHITE. IT HAS BLINDS OF DARK GREEN,
AND ROOF OF WOOD SHINGLES STAINED TO A WEATHERED GRAY. THE HOUSE IS 33' x 36'
OVER ALL, AND FACES EAST

FIRST FLOOR PLAN

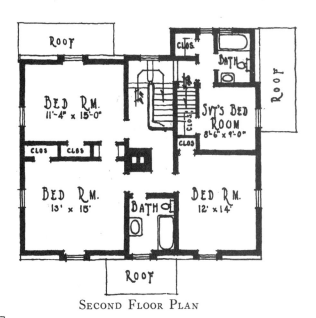

SECOND FLOOR PLAN

The House of James H. Cleaves, Esq.

Henry Atherton Frost & Eleanor Raymond, Architects

A PICKET FENCE ENCLOSES THE LAWN IN FRONT OF THE MAIN PART OF THE HOUSE

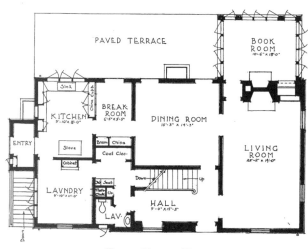

FIRST FLOOR PLAN

SECOND FLOOR PLAN

THIS HOUSE IN WINCHESTER, MASSACHUSETTS, HAS
EXTERIOR WALLS OF MATCHED BOARDS OR SHIP-LAP,
PAINTED A PEARL GRAY, WHILE THE DOORWAY AND
BLINDS, WITH HEAVY, WIDELY-SPACED SLATS, ARE
WHITE. THE SERVICE END OF THE HOUSE, WHICH IS
SLIGHTLY RECESSED, HAS WALLS OF GRAY SHINGLES,
AND IS FURTHER SET OFF FROM THE MAIN BODY OF
THE HOUSE BY THE FENCE WHICH JOINS THE HOUSE
AT THE BREAK IN THE FAÇADE. THE PLAN, AN UN-
USUALLY CONVENIENT ONE, WAS ESPECIALLY DE-
SIGNED FOR A SERVANTLESS HOUSEHOLD

AT THE RIGHT IS A DETAIL OF THE DOORWAY, SHOWING
ITS RATHER HEAVY, CLASSIC TREATMENT, WHICH,
WITH THE BLINDS, GIVES THE HOUSE ITS STURDY
CHARACTER. THE DOOR ITSELF IS PAINTED MITIS
GREEN. THE PHOTOGRAPH BELOW SHOWS THE BOOK-
ROOM AND SLEEPING PORCH, AND GIVES A GLIMPSE
OF THE SCREENED TERRACE ON TO WHICH THE DINING
ROOM AND BOOKROOM OPEN. THE SCREENED SIDES
ENCLOSING THIS TERRACE ARE ENTIRELY REMOVABLE,
SO THAT IN WINTER NO SUNLIGHT IS LOST TO THE
ROOMS ON THE REAR, WHICH FACE SOUTH

THE HOUSE OF CHARLES E. GREENE, ESQ.

Derby & Robinson, Architects

THE HOUSE FACES EAST ON A LEVEL AND WELL-WOODED LOT

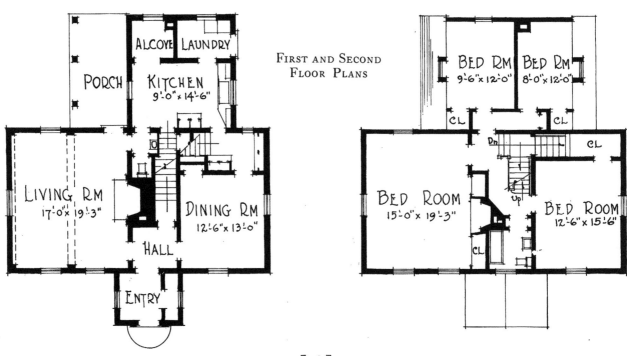

FIRST AND SECOND
FLOOR PLANS

PORCH

ALCOVE LAUNDRY

KITCHEN
9'-0" x 14'-6"

LIVING RM
17'-0" x 19'-3"

DINING RM
12'-6" x 13'-0"

HALL

ENTRY

BED RM
9'-6" x 12'-0"

BED RM
8'-0" x 12'-0"

CL

CL

CL

Dn

Up

BED ROOM
15'-0" x 19'-3"

BED ROOM
12'-6" x 15'-6"

CL

THIS COLONIAL HOUSE IN WINCHESTER, MAS-
SACHUSETTS, EXCELLENTLY PRESERVES THE
SPIRIT OF THE OLD WITHOUT BEING IN ANY WAY
A COPY OF A PARTICULAR HOUSE. THE EXTERIOR
WALLS ARE OF NARROW CLAPBOARDS WEATH—
ERED BROWN, THE TRIM IS OF CYPRESS ALSO
WEATHERED BROWN, AND THE ROOF IS OF
WEATHERED SHINGLES. THE PLAN IS PARTIC-
ULARLY INTERESTING BECAUSE IT SHOWS HOW
WELL THIS TYPE OF HOUSE CAN BE ADAPTED TO
MODERN IDEAS OF COMFORT AND CONVENIENCE

AT THE RIGHT IS A DETAIL OF THE REAR ELL,
WHICH HAS CHARACTERISTIC GAMBREL ROOF,
SMALL-PANED WINDOWS, AND WOODEN GUT-
TERS. BELOW IS A VIEW OF THE LIVING ROOM,
SHOWING WALLS OF CREAM PLASTER AND THE
FEATHER-EDGE PINE BOARDING, THE HEAVY
BEAM CONSTRUCTION, AND THE SIMPLE TRIM
TYPICAL OF THE EARLY HOUSES OF NEW
ENGLAND

The House of George H. Taber, Jr., Esq.

Woolsey & Chapman, Architects

THIS HOUSE FACES WEST AND IS IN RYE, NEW YORK

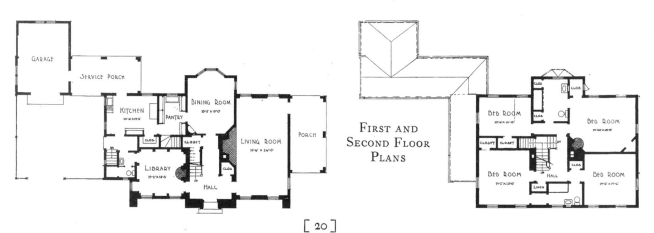

FIRST AND
SECOND FLOOR
PLANS

THE HOUSE PRESENTS AN INTERESTING VARIATION FROM THE COLONIAL IN ITS USE OF WHITEWASHED STONE
WITH THE WHITE HAND-RIVEN CYPRESS SHINGLES, BUT ADHERES TO TYPE IN ITS EXCELLENT WINDOW AND DOOR
DETAIL. THE ROOF IS OF CEDAR SHINGLES IN VARIEGATED COLORS

THE HOUSE OF MRS. MARIE C. TUSSEY

Leslie I. Nichols, Architect

A HOUSE OF SIMPLE ENGLISH COTTAGE TYPE IN LARCHMONT, NEW YORK

FIRST FLOOR PLAN

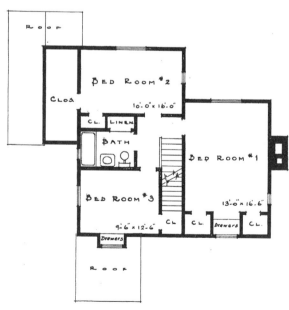

SECOND FLOOR PLAN

THE STUCCO WALLS OF THIS HOUSE HAVE BEEN
GIVEN TWO COATS OF WHITEWASH IN WHICH
HAVE BEEN MIXED VARYING AMOUNTS OF YEL-
LOW OCHRE, WHILE THE SIDING OF CEDAR HAS
BEEN GIVEN TWO COATS OF LINSEED OIL. THE
HOUSE IS SITUATED ON A LOT 75′ X 115′, TWO
FEET BELOW THE STREET LEVEL, CHOSEN
LARGELY BECAUSE OF A VENERABLE OAK. THE
PLAN HAS BEEN WORKED OUT ESPECIALLY WITH
REGARD TO EASE OF HOUSEKEEPING, AND WAS
DETERMINED FIRST BY THE POINTS OF THE
COMPASS, THE LIVING ROOM AND DINING ROOM
FACING SOUTH AND WEST, AND THE GARAGE
AND MAID'S ROOM NORTH

AT THE RIGHT IS A VIEW OF THE LIVING ROOM
FIREPLACE, AND BELOW FRONT AND SIDE
VIEWS OF THE HOUSE, SHOWING THE GARAGE.
THE INTERIOR IS CHARACTERIZED BY THE
SIMPLICITY OF THE EARLIEST NEW ENGLAND
HOUSES, AS IS SEEN IN THE BEAMS OF HAND-
HEWN OAK AND THE WALLS OF WIDE, VERTICAL
PINE BOARDS. THE FLOORS ALSO ARE OF WIDE
PINE BOARDS. ALL THE DOORS OF MATCHED
WOOD WERE MADE ON THE JOB, AND ON THE
FIRST FLOOR THEY HAVE WOODEN LATCHES

The House of Albert Guinn Hope, Esq.

John F. Staub, Architect

THIS HOUSE OF ENGLISH COTTAGE TYPE WAS BUILT IN KNOXVILLE, TENNESSEE. IT HAS
CONCRETE FOUNDATIONS, WALLS OF WOOD FRAME COVERED WITH STUCCO ON WIRE LATH,
TRIM OF ANTIQUE OAK WEATHERED, AND A ROOF OF SLATE OF VARIED SIZE AND THICK-
NESS, RANGING FROM BLUISH GREEN TO PURPLE, WITH A LITTLE OF THE GRAY AND
NATURAL COLOR

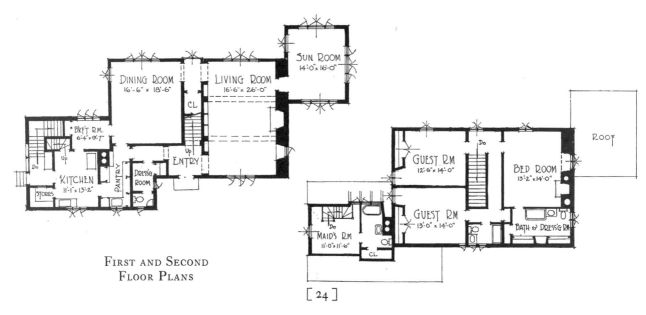

First and Second
Floor Plans

THE STUCCO WALLS ARE GRAY IN COLOR, AND THE WINDOW AND DOOR FRAMES ARE PAINTED A ROBIN'S-EGG BLUE.
ALL THE LIVING ROOMS FACE SOUTH, AND LOOK OUT UPON THIS GARDEN OF NARROW TERRACES AND DRY-LAID
RETAINING WALLS

TWO VIEWS OF THE LIVING ROOM OF THE HOPE HOUSE ARE SHOWN ON THIS PAGE: THE
WEST WALL (ABOVE) WHICH HAS BEEN FURRED OUT TO THE DEPTH OF THE CHIMNEY,
SO GIVING A DEEP REVEAL TO THE WINDOW, AND THE EAST WALL (BELOW) WHICH IS
PANELED WITH BOOKSHELVES. THE WALLS AND CEILING OF THIS ROOM ARE OF NAT-
URAL-COLOR PLASTER, WHILE THE WOODWORK IS OF ANTIQUE OAK WEATHERED. ALL
OF THE EXPOSED TIMBER IN THIS ROOM IS STRUCTURAL. IT WAS FOUND IN AN OLD
BARN AND HAS BEEN GIVEN NO OTHER TREATMENT THAN WASHING

THE HOUSE OF ALBERT KLAMROTH, ESQ.

Holmes & Von Schmid, Architects

OF FRENCH COTTAGE TYPE, THIS HOUSE IS LOCATED IN ESSEX FELLS, NEW JERSEY.
IT IS OF WARM GRAY STUCCO ON WOOD FRAME, WITH EXTERIOR TRIM OF OAK WEATH-
ERED BROWN, AND ROOF OF SHINGLES IN AUTUMN COLORS. IT WAS DESIGNED AS A
SERVANTLESS HOUSE FOR A MAN AND HIS DAUGHTER

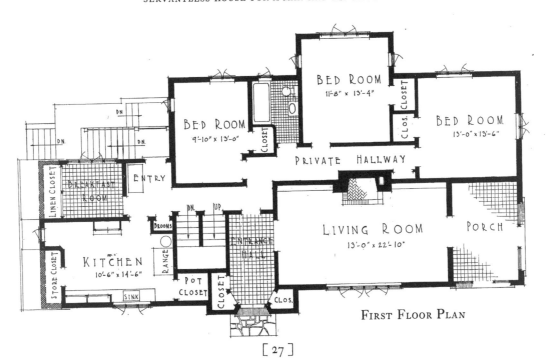

FIRST FLOOR PLAN

THE HOUSE OF J. H. JEWETT, ESQ.

Lewis Bowman, Architect

A HOUSE IN BRONXVILLE, NEW YORK, OF STUCCO OF A FAINT PINK HUE ON HOLLOW
TILE. THE ROOF IS OF WOOD SHINGLES WEATHERED GRAY. THE HOUSE IS OF SIMPLE
COTTAGE CHARACTER, WITH NO EXTERIOR WOOD TRIM AND VERY LITTLE WOODWORK
INSIDE, THE WALLS BEING PRINCIPALLY OF WHITE ROUGH PLASTER

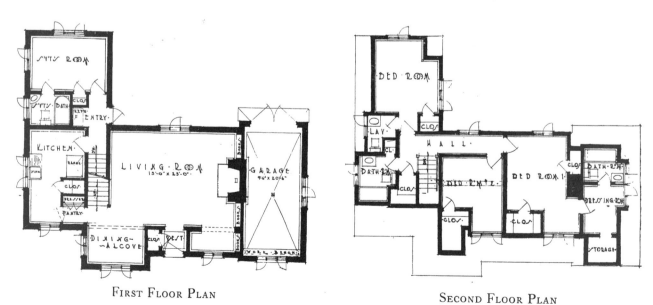

FIRST FLOOR PLAN   SECOND FLOOR PLAN

THE HOUSE OF J. F. SHEETZ, ESQ.

Lewis Bowman, Architect

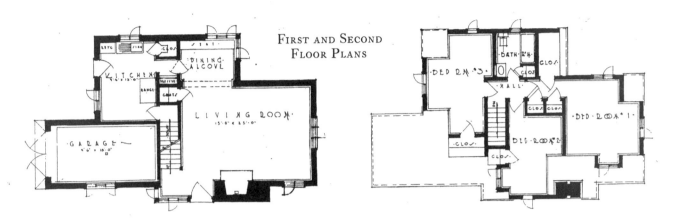

FIRST AND SECOND
FLOOR PLANS

THIS HOUSE IS ALSO IN BRONXVILLE, NEW YORK, AND LIKE THE ONE ON THE PRECEDING PAGE, IS OF STUCCO ON HOLLOW TILE. IN THIS CASE, THE STUCCO IS CREAM COLOR. EACH OF THESE COTTAGES IS APPROPRIATELY PLACED IN AN OLD APPLE ORCHARD, AND BOTH ARE FORTUNATE IN THE TREATMENT OF THEIR GROUNDS

The House of J. E. Crawford, Esq.

Marston, Van Pelt & Maybury, Architects

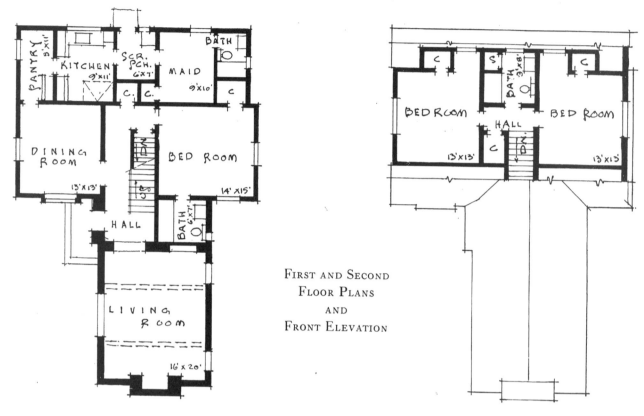

First and Second
Floor Plans
and
Front Elevation

THIS HOUSE WAS DESIGNED FOR THOMAS & STEPHENSON, WHO BUILT IT IN PASADENA, CALIFORNIA. IT IS OF WHITE STUCCO ON WOOD FRAME, WITH EXTERIOR TRIM OF REDWOOD AND OREGON PINE WHICH HAS BEEN ALLOWED TO WEATHER. THE SASHES ARE PAINTED BLUE-GREEN, AS IS ALSO THE DOOR, WITH ITS DECORATIVE WROUGHT-IRON HINGES. THE ROOF IS OF ROYAL CEDAR SHINGLES IN NATURAL COLOR, AND THE CASEMENTS THROUGHOUT ARE OF STEEL. INSIDE, THE WALLS ARE OF HAND-FINISHED KEENE'S CEMENT, WHICH HAS BEEN GIVEN A TONE SLIGHTLY OFF WHITE BY THE USE OF UMBER

The House of Richard E. Bishop, Esq.

Edmund B. Gilchrist, Architect

THE CURVING STAIR HAS THE INTERESTING WINDOW TREATMENT SHOWN ABOVE

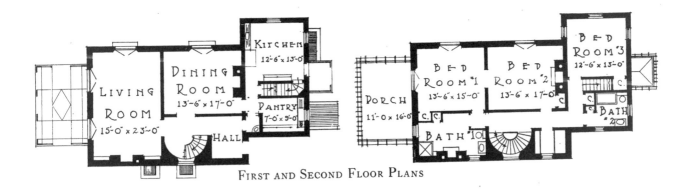

FIRST AND SECOND FLOOR PLANS

THIS HOUSE IN GERMAN-
TOWN, PENNSYLVANIA, IS
BUILT OF BRICK, COVERED
WITH ROUGH-CAST STUCCO
TONED A LIGHT WARM GRAY.
THE EXTERIOR TRIM IS
PAINTED WHITE; THE DOOR
AND SHUTTERS ARE DARK
GREEN. THE ROOF IS OF
SLATE IN VARYING TONES OF
GRAY, BLUE, AND GREEN.
THE CHIMNEYS HAVE BEEN
GIVEN A COAT OF WHITE-
WASH WHICH HAS PARTIALLY
PEELED OFF, LEAVING A
PLEASING MOTTLED COLOR.
ON AXIS WITH THE FRENCH
DOOR IN THE LIVING ROOM
IS A GARDEN PATH, LEADING
TO A CIRCULAR POOL

The House of Karl W. Bradley, Esq.

Karl W. Bradley, Architect

THIS HOUSE, OF ENGLISH COTTAGE TYPE, FACES SOUTHEAST ON A SOMEWHAT IRREGULAR AND BEAUTIFULLY WOODED
LOT IN SCARSDALE, NEW YORK

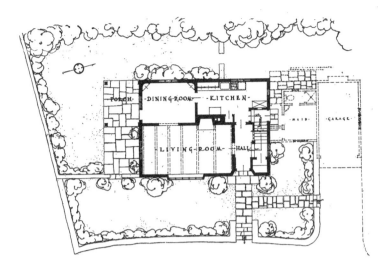

The First and Second Floor Plans

THE PARTS OF THE PLANS DRAWN IN DASH LINES INDICATE FUTURE ADDITIONS TO THE HOUSE: ON THE FIRST FLOOR A MAID'S ROOM, BATH, AND ATTACHED GARAGE, AND ON THE SECOND FLOOR A BEDROOM AND BATH WHICH WILL BE REACHED FROM THE STAIR LANDING

THE EXTERIOR WALLS ARE OF BUFF-SALMON-PINK STUCCO ON WOOD FRAME AND THE HOUSE AS NOW BUILT IS 24' X 34' OVER ALL. THE EXTERIOR TRIM IS OF WHITE PINE WEATHERED BROWN; THE ROOF IS OF HEAVY IRREGULAR SLATE IN TONES OF BLACK, PURPLE, AND BROWN; THE LEADED CASEMENTS HAVE ANTIQUE LAC GLASS IN DELICATE TONES OF GREEN, AMBER, AND PALE YELLOW

AT THE RIGHT IS A VIEW OF THE STAIRWAY, SEEN THROUGH THE ARCHED DOOR IN THE LIVING ROOM. ALL THE INTERIOR WOODWORK IS WHITE PINE, WHICH HAS BEEN GIVEN THE APPEARANCE OF OLD WOOD; THE WALLS ARE OF PLASTER, TONED A WARM SMOKY GRAY, AND THE FLOORS ARE OF WIDE OAK PLANKS

[35]

IN BOTH THE DINING ROOM AND THE LIVING ROOM OF THE BRADLEY HOUSE, THE SAME COLOR SCHEME OF BLUE-GREEN WITH TOUCHES OF RED HAS BEEN USED. THE FURNITURE, MUCH OF IT ANCESTRAL, IS OF COTTAGE TYPE APPROPRIATE FOR THE HOUSE. THE CUPBOARDS IN THE DINING ROOM ARE PAINTED ON THE INSIDE A CHINESE VERMILION

THE HOUSE OF STEPHEN PICHETTO, ESQ.

Dwight James Baum, Architect

BUILT OF WOOD FRAME WHICH IS COVERED WITH METAL LATH AND STUCCO OF CREAM
COLOR, THIS HOUSE IS LOCATED IN FIELDSTON, NEW YORK. THE TRIM, ALSO OF CREAM,
HAS A SANDED FINISH. THE ROOF IS OF WOOD SHINGLES STAINED BROWN, AND THE
DOOR AND THE SLATTED BLINDS ARE BOTH GREEN. IN ADDITION TO THE FOUR BED-
ROOMS AND TWO BATHS ON THE SECOND FLOOR, THERE IS SPACE FOR ONE ROOM AND
A BATH ON THE THIRD FLOOR

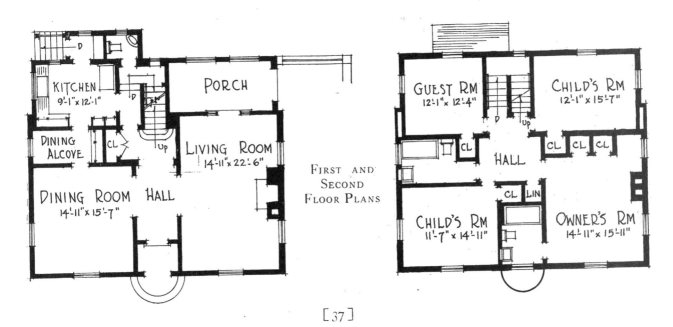

FIRST AND
SECOND
FLOOR PLANS

THE HOUSE OF FRANK J. FORSTER, ESQ.

Frank J. Forster, Architect

THIS HOUSE, OF NORMAN TYPE, FACES SOUTH ON A WOODLAND LOT IN GREAT NECK, LONG ISLAND

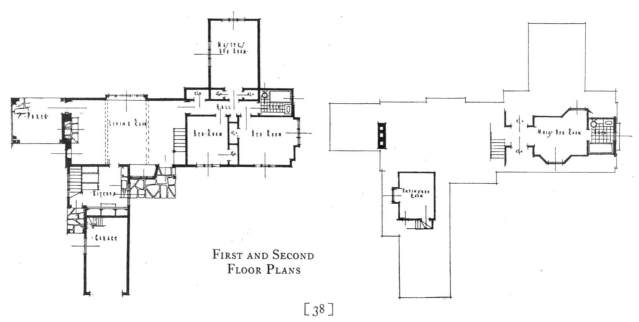

FIRST AND SECOND
FLOOR PLANS

THE HOUSE IS OF WHITE-WASHED
STUCCO ON WOOD FRAME,
WITH EXTERIOR TRIM OF SOLID
OAK WEATHERED A GRAYISH
BROWN, AND ROOF OF SLATE IN
WEATHERED GREEN TONES. IN-
CLUDING THE PROJECTING ELLS,
ITS OVER-ALL DIMENSIONS ARE
64' 3" X 61' 8". AT THE RIGHT
IS A VIEW OF THE WINDOW ON
THE NORTH SIDE OF THE LIVING
ROOM, AND BELOW, THE WEST
ELEVATION OF THE HOUSE,
SHOWING SERVICE ENTRANCE
AND LIVING PORCH

AS THE HOUSE HAS NO HALL
AND NO DINING ROOM, THE
LIVING ROOM SERVES ALSO THE
PURPOSES OF THESE ROOMS.
THIS COMBINATION LIVING
ROOM AND DINING ROOM IS TWO
STORIES IN HEIGHT; IT HAS
WALLS AND CEILING OF
MOTTLED PLASTER OF A SMOKY
GRAY COLOR, AND WOODWORK
OF SOLID OAK

THE HOUSE OF CHESTER LINDSAY CHURCHILL, ESQ.

Chester Lindsay Churchill, Architect

THE HOUSE FACES WEST ON A SLOPING LOT IN WABAN, MASSACHUSETTS

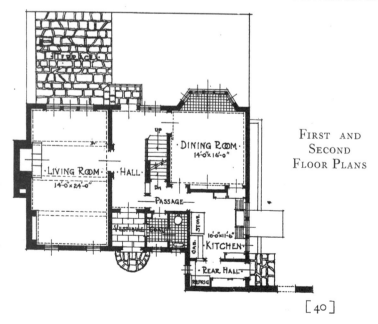

FIRST AND
SECOND
FLOOR PLANS

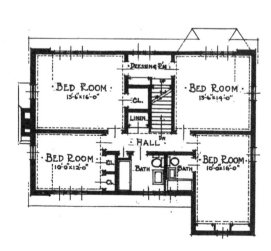

THE HOUSE IS OF STUCCO OF WARM
CREAM COLOR IN A ROUGH ENGLISH
TEXTURE, WITH FRONT DOOR OF OAK
WHICH THE TRIM IS STAINED TO MATCH.
THE ROOF IS OF SLATE WITH GRADUATED
COURSES VARYING IN COLOR. SINCE THE
PLANS WERE DRAWN, A GARAGE HAS BEEN
ADDED AT THE REAR, ONE SIDE WALL OF
WHICH CONTINUES TO THE HOUSE AS A
FREE STANDING WALL, AS THE PHOTO-
GRAPH BELOW SHOWS

THE WALLS INSIDE ARE OF A WARM-
TONED PLASTER OF UNEVEN TEXTURE,
BUT FINISHED SMOOTH WITH A SLIGHT
POLISH. THE WOODWORK IS OAK, AND IN
THE HALL IS A WROUGHT-IRON STAIR-
RAIL. THE LIVING ROOM IS TWO STEPS
BELOW THE HALL, AND HAS LONG WIN-
DOWS WITH TRIPLE-HUNG SASHES, WHICH
ARE SO ARRANGED THAT, BY LIFTING THE
LOWER TWO, EXIT MAY BE GAINED TO THE
PAVED TERRACE AT THE REAR

A House in Chestnut Hill, Massachusetts

Gordon Allen, Architect

THIS HOUSE WAS DESIGNED FOR ONE WOMAN, WHO INTENDED TO LIVE ALONE IN IT WITH ONE MAID, AND A STUDY OF THE PLANS SHOWS THAT IT IS WELL ARRANGED FOR SUCH A PURPOSE. THE LARGE HALL, FROM WHICH THE STAIRS ARE SHUT OFF BY A DOOR, SERVES AS A SECOND LIVING ROOM, AND THE LIVING ROOM PROPER IS USED ALSO AS A DINING ROOM. ON THE SECOND FLOOR, THE RELATIVE SIZES OF DRESSING ROOM AND BEDROOM ARE UNUSUAL, THE DRESSING ROOM AS HERE PLANNED BEING LARGE ENOUGH TO SERVE AS AN UPSTAIRS SITTING ROOM WITH A SEPARATE DOOR FROM THE HALL, AND THE BEDROOM REDUCED TO AN AREA ONLY LARGE ENOUGH TO CONTAIN A BED AND BUREAU

FIRST FLOOR PLAN   SECOND FLOOR PLAN

THE HALL, AS SHOWN AT THE LEFT, HAS A TILE FLOOR AND GRAY PLASTER WALLS, WITH TRIM OF PINE ALSO GRAY. THE OUTSIDE WALL HAS BEEN FURRED TO PROVIDE BOOKSHELVES AND A WIDE WINDOW LEDGE, GIVING THE EFFECT FROM WITHIN OF A THICK MASONRY WALL

THE WALLS OF THE HOUSE ARE OF SMOOTH-FINISH PINK STUCCO ON WOOD FRAME, AND THE ROOF IS OF ANTIQUE TILES IN SOFT RED, BROUGHT FROM PENNSYLVANIA. THE SIMPLE DOOR HAS AN INTERESTING ENFRAMEMENT OF STUCCO, MADE TO SIMULATE QUOINS. IN FRONT OF THE HOUSE IS A FLAGGED TERRACE, RETAINED BY A STONE WALL

THE HOUSE OF GEORGE S. HUNT, ESQ.

Marston, Van Pelt & Maybury, Architects

THIS HOUSE IN PASADENA, CALIFORNIA, RECEIVED THE FIRST PRIZE IN A COMPETITION HELD IN 1925 BY THE HOUSE BEAUTIFUL PUBLISHING CORPORATION, AS THE BEST HOUSE BUILT WEST OF THE MISSISSIPPI SINCE 1921. THE HOUSE OF SCOTCH PEASANT TYPE IS OF OYSTER-WHITE STUCCO ON WOOD FRAME; THE EXTERIOR TRIM IS STAINED BROWN, AND THE ROOF HAS EXTRA-SIZED WOODEN SHINGLES OF THREE TONES OF BROWN, LAID SLIGHTLY UNEVENLY. THE HOUSE FACES EAST

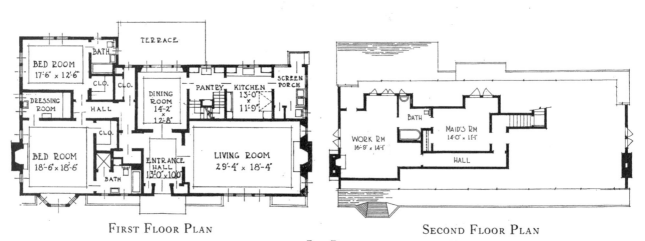

FIRST FLOOR PLAN   SECOND FLOOR PLAN

THE DEEPLY RECESSED DOORWAY, WITH
DOOR OF RICH BROWN, HAS A SIMPLE
PLASTER MOULDING FOR ENFRAMEMENT,
AS THE PHOTOGRAPH ON THE LEFT SHOWS

THE LIVING ROOM HAS A COVE CEILING
AND SIMPLY CARVED BEAMS. ITS WALLS
ARE OF PARCHMENT-COLORED PLASTER,
AND THE WOODWORK IS OF OREGON
PINE STAINED THE COLOR OF WALNUT.
THE LARGE WINDOW AND FRENCH DOORS
IN THE LIVING ROOM MAKE A PLEASANT
FEATURE, WHICH IS BALANCED ON THE
OUTSIDE BY THE BAY WINDOW IN THE
BEDROOM. THESE TWO ACCENTING NOTES
GIVE A HAPPY RHYTHM TO THE FAÇADE,
WHICH WITHOUT THEM MIGHT HAVE
PROVED MONOTONOUS

THE HOUSE OF LESTER G. BALDWIN, ESQ.

George Washington Smith, Architect

A HOUSE IN PASADENA, CALIFORNIA, DISTINCTLY OF THE SPANISH TYPE, BOTH IN ITS
GENERAL PROPORTIONS AND IN SUCH DETAILS AS ITS IRON GRILLES AND BALCONIES.
THE LONG, UNBROKEN LINE OF THE ROOF AND THE LARGE WALL SPACES ARE ALSO
CHARACTERISTIC, AND THE SLIGHT OVERHANG OF THE SECOND STORY, SUPPORTED ON
PROJECTING BEAMS, A HAPPY FEATURE

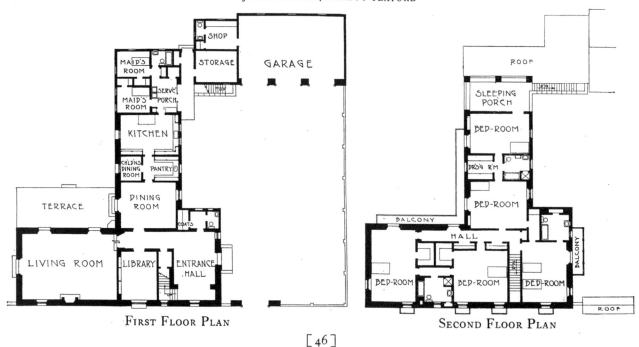

FIRST FLOOR PLAN

SECOND FLOOR PLAN

THE HOUSE IS OF WOOD-FRAME CONSTRUCTION WITH A FINISH OF WHITE STUCCO AND A ROOF OF TILE. AT THE LEFT IS A VIEW OF THE GARDEN AND PAVED TERRACE ON WHICH THE LIVING ROOM OPENS, AND OF A PART OF THE BALCONY ON THE SECOND FLOOR, WHICH CONNECTS THREE OF THE PRINCIPAL BEDROOMS. ALL THE BEDROOMS HAVE AT LEAST ONE PAIR OF FRENCH DOORS, AND SEVERAL OF THEM MORE; THUS THEY ARE ENSURED PLENTY OF LIGHT AND AIR. THE PHOTOGRAPH BELOW SHOWS THE COVERED GATEWAY TO THE ENTRANCE COURT AND ONE OF THE POINTED ARCHED DOORWAYS TO THE GARAGE

THE HOUSE OF GEORGE H. CUTTER, ESQ.

Dean & Dean, Architects

THIS HOUSE OF PUTTY-COLORED STUCCO ON
WOOD FRAME IS LOCATED IN SACRAMENTO,
CALIFORNIA. IT IS BUILT ON A CORNER LOT,
FACING NORTH. THE EXTERIOR TRIM IS OF PINE
PAINTED A LIGHT BROWN, AND THE ROOF IS OF
VARICOLORED CEDAR SHINGLES

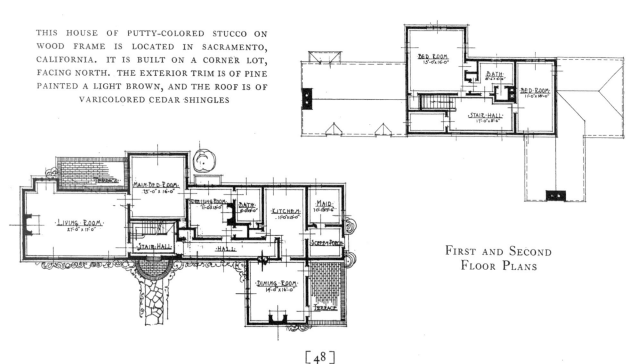

FIRST AND SECOND
FLOOR PLANS

THE LIVING ROOM IN THE ELL AT THE LEFT OF THE MAIN ENTRANCE IS OPEN TO THE ROOF. IT HAS ATTRACTIVE
CASEMENT WINDOWS ON THE FRONT, AND A BAY WINDOW AND FRENCH DOORS OPENING ON THE REAR TERRACE

The House of Robert M. Haig, Esq.

Julius Gregory, Architect

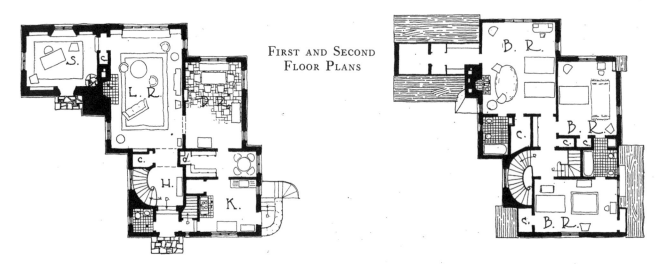

FIRST AND SECOND
FLOOR PLANS

SITUATED IN RIVERDALE, NEW YORK, THIS ENGLISH COTTAGE HAS WALLS OF HOLLOW
TILE COVERED WITH GRAY STUCCO. THE EXTERIOR TRIM IS OF OAK STAINED GRAY;
THE ROOF IS OF WOOD SHINGLES, MOTTLED BROWN IN COLOR, AND LAID WITH A
NARROW EXPOSURE TO THE WEATHER. THE HOUSE, 44′ X 52′ OVER ALL, FACES EAST

A House in Pasadena, California

Roland E. Coate, Architect

THIS HOUSE SUGGESTS THE EARLY ADOBE HOUSES
OF CALIFORNIA, AND IS A CHARMING ADAPTATION
OF THAT TYPE. IT IS OF WOOD-FRAME CONSTRUC-
TION, WITH A STUCCO FINISH WHITE IN COLOR.
THE VERTICAL LINES OF THE BALUSTERS OF THE
SIMPLE WOODEN BALCONY, WHICH IS ALSO WHITE,
ARE REPEATED IN THE PICKETS OF THE FENCE, AND
MAKE A PATTERN WHICH IS PLEASINGLY INTER-
RUPTED BY THE TWO PEPPER TREES

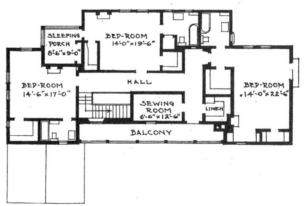

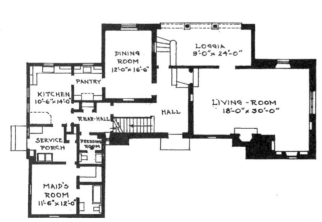

First and Second
Floor Plans

THE HOUSE OF THOMAS J. ACKISS, ESQ.

Edgar & Verna Cook Salomonsky, Architects

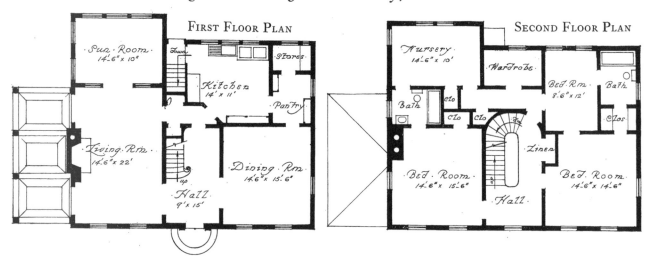

FIRST FLOOR PLAN

SECOND FLOOR PLAN

BUILT IN NORFOLK, VIRGINIA, THIS HOUSE OF WHITE STUCCO ON WOOD FRAME HAS THE
CHARACTER OF THE LOCAL COLONIAL ARCHITECTURE. THE EXTERIOR TRIM IS WHITE;
THE DOOR AND SHUTTERS ON THE FIRST FLOOR ARE ALSO WHITE; THE BLINDS ON THE
SECOND FLOOR ARE GREEN. THE ROOF IS OF SLATE, VERY DARK GRAY IN COLOR

IN BOTH THE HALL AND LIVING ROOM
THE WALLS ARE PLASTER, PAINTED
CREAM COLOR, AND THE WOODWORK
WHITE PINE, PAINTED THE SAME SHADE.
THE REFINEMENT THAT IS FOUND IN THE
EXTERIOR DETAIL OF THE HOUSE IS SEEN
ALSO INSIDE IN THE SIMPLICITY OF THE
STAIRCASE AND THE REPEATING CURVE
OF THE DOOR, AND IN THE TREATMENT OF
THE FIREPLACE IN THE LIVING ROOM.

[53]

The House of William Gehron, Esq.

William Gehron, Architect

THIS HOUSE IN PELHAM, NEW YORK, IS BUILT ON A LOT FACING WEST. IT IS OF HOLLOW
TILE COVERED WITH STUCCO OF A LIGHT WARM GRAY COLOR. THE ROOF IS OF GREEN
AND PURPLE SLATE; THE CORNICE OF WOOD AND THE SHUTTERS ON THE SECOND FLOOR
ARE PAINTED WHITE. ON THE FIRST FLOOR ARE STEEL CASEMENTS WHICH HAVE TILE
SILLS BOTH INSIDE AND OUT, WHILE ON THE SECOND FLOOR THE WINDOWS ARE DOUBLE-
HUNG. THERE IS SPACE FOR ONE BEDROOM AND A BATH ON THE THIRD FLOOR

FIRST FLOOR PLAN

SECOND FLOOR PLAN

THE DETAIL OF THIS HOUSE SUGGESTS BOTH ITALY AND SPAIN, AND YET THE HOUSE IS DISTINCTLY AMERICAN

The House of F. Stoddard Smith, Esq.

Holmes & Von Schmid, Architects

THIS HOUSE OF ENGLISH COTTAGE TYPE HAS WALLS OF WARM TAN STUCCO ON WOOD FRAME, WITH HALF-TIMBER CONSTRUCTION OF LIGHT STAINED OAK, AND UNPLANED OAK IN THE GABLES OVER THE SECOND-STORY WINDOWS. THE ROOF IS OF HEAVY SLATE IN VARIEGATED COLORS. THE HOUSE, 28' x 50' OVER ALL, FACES WEST. IT IS IN MONTCLAIR, NEW JERSEY

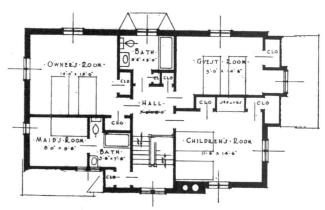

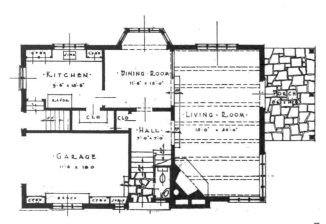

FIRST AND SECOND
FLOOR PLANS

AT THE RIGHT IS A VIEW OF THE FRONT
ELEVATION AND GARAGE END OF THE
HOUSE. THE CHIMNEY, WHICH IS OF
PLEASING DESIGN AND TEXTURE, IS OF
HARD-BURNED BRICK IRREGULARLY LAID.
BRICK ALSO APPEARS IN HERRINGBONE
PATTERN IN A PANEL UNDER THE WINDOW
AT THE RIGHT OF THE ENTRANCE DOOR.
AT THE CORNER OF THE GARAGE, A
CONCRETE WATER BARREL HAS FLOWER
POTS SET AROUND ITS BASE

BELOW IS A VIEW OF THE LIVING ROOM
AND DINING ROOM. THE WALLS INSIDE
ARE OF ROUGH PLASTER, SOFT BROWN IN
TONE, AND THE WOODWORK, INCLUDING
THE BEAMS, IS OF DARK BROWN OAK.
THE DOORS ARE OF SIMPLE PLANK CON-
STRUCTION. THE LOWER STEPS TO THE
DINING ROOM AND TO THE HALL ARE
SOLID OAK BEAMS

THE HOUSE OF HUGH KAHLER, ESQ.

Aymar Embury II, Architect

THIS HOUSE IS LOCATED IN PRINCETON, NEW JERSEY. IT IS OF WOOD-FRAME CONSTRUCTION, COVERED WITH A CREAM-COLORED, SMOOTH-TEXTURED STUCCO. THE EXTERIOR TRIM IS OF CHESTNUT; THE ROOF OF SLATE, ONE HALF VARIEGATED GREEN AND PURPLE, THE REST PLAIN GREEN AND PLAIN PURPLE IN EQUAL AMOUNT

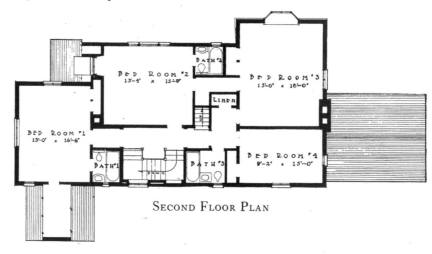

SECOND FLOOR PLAN

FIRST FLOOR PLAN

IN THIS HOUSE LEDGE STONE
HAS BEEN SUCCESSFULLY COM-
BINED WITH STUCCO. IT IS
USED AT THE CORNERS OF THE
ELL CONTAINING THE MAID'S
ROOM, IN ONE CHIMNEY, AND
IN THE END OF THE ELL CON-
TAINING THE STUDY. THE PHO-
TOGRAPH AT THE LEFT SHOWS
THAT A WINDOW IN THE FIRE-
PLACE SIDE OF THE LIVING
ROOM, OVERLOOKING THE PAVED
TERRACE, HAS REPLACED THE
DOOR SHOWN ON THE PLAN

AT THE RIGHT AND ABOVE
ARE VIEWS SHOWING THE
END AND REAR SIDE OF THE
STUDY ELL

THE HOUSE OF MRS. M. L. H. WALKER

Wallace Neff, Architect

THIS HOUSE OF WHITE STUCCO IN PASADENA, CALIFORNIA, RECEIVED IN THE 1923 AWARDS A CERTIFICATE OF HONOR FROM THE SOUTHERN CALIFORNIA CHAPTER OF THE AMERICAN INSTITUTE OF ARCHITECTS, FOR THE BEST SINGLE DETACHED DWELLING OF THIRTEEN ROOMS OR LESS. THE HOUSE SHOWS AN INTERESTING USE OF SPANISH MOTIVES WHICH HAVE BEEN INCORPORATED SUCCESSFULLY IN THE DESIGN, WHILE THE SEVERITY AND PLAINNESS OF THE SPANISH HOUSE HAVE BEEN AVOIDED. A COVERED WOODEN BALCONY CONNECTS A MAIN BEDROOM WITH THE SLEEPING PORCH, AND A SMALLER BALCONY OPENS FROM THIS SOUTH BEDROOM ON THE OPPOSITE SIDE

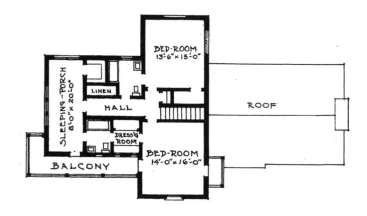

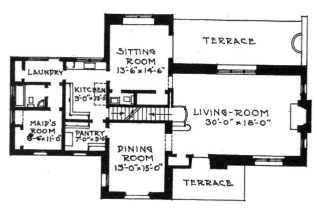

FIRST AND SECOND
FLOOR PLANS

A House in Larchmont, New York

Sherrill Whiton, Architect

THIS COTTAGE OF NORMANDY FARMHOUSE TYPE IS BUILT OF CONCRETE BLOCKS, 8″ X 8″ X 12″ IN SIZE AND FINISHED IN A SMOOTH NATURAL COLOR. IT HAS RED BRICK TRIM AND A ROOF OF GREEN VARIEGATED SLATE. INSIDE THE WALLS ARE FURRED, AND PLASTERED IN A NATURAL YELLOW TONE WITH ROUGH TEXTURE. THIS TYPE OF CONSTRUCTION FOR THIS HOUSE COST ABOUT TEN PER CENT MORE THAN WOOD CONSTRUCTION WOULD HAVE. THE HOUSE, 25′ X 26′ OVER ALL, FACES NORTH

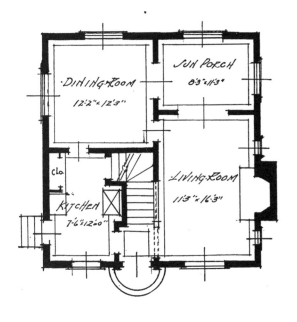

FIRST
AND
SECOND
FLOOR
PLANS

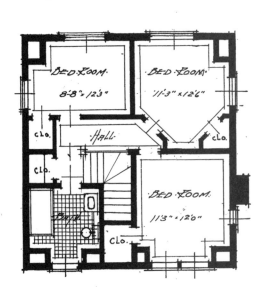

THE HOUSE OF WALLACE FROST, ESQ.

Wallace Frost, Architect

THIS HOUSE OF CONCRETE BLOCKS, WHITEWASHED, WAS
BUILT IN BIRMINGHAM, MICHIGAN. IT HAS SILLS, LINTELS,
AND BEAMS OF OLD MILL TIMBERS OF VERY DARK COLOR.
THE ROOF IS OF DARK WOOD SHINGLES; THE CHIMNEYS OF
BRICK ARE WHITEWASHED. THE HOUSE IS APPROXI-
MATELY 40' X 65' AND FACES SOUTH

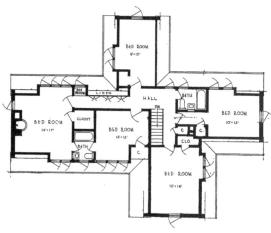

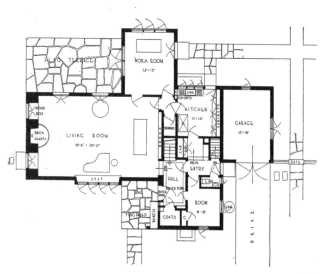

FIRST AND SECOND
FLOOR PLANS

ABOVE IS A VIEW OF THE FRONT OF THE HOUSE, WHICH SHOWS THE ENTRANCE TO THE
GARAGE ON THE RIGHT. BELOW IS THE WEST END OF THE HOUSE, WITH A TERRACE ON
THE LEFT BETWEEN LIVING ROOM AND WORKROOM

THE HOUSE OF KARL KEFFER, ESQ.

Frank J. Forster, Architect

A HOUSE OF EXCELLENT LINES AND PLEASING TEXTURE IN SCARSDALE, NEW YORK

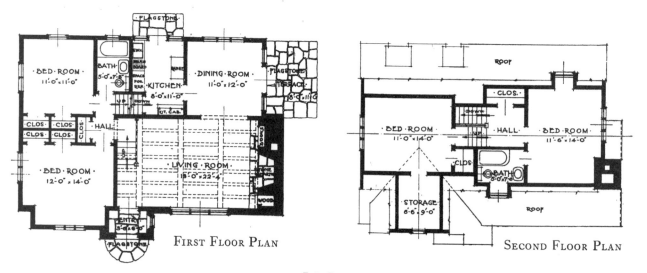

FIRST FLOOR PLAN

SECOND FLOOR PLAN

THE HOUSE IS OF WOOD-FRAME CONSTRUCTION, COVERED WITH STUCCO EXCEPT FOR THE ENTRANCE GABLE AND
FACE, WHICH ARE OF BRICK, AND THE END OF THE LIVING-ROOM WALL, WHICH IS OF BRICK AND STONE LAID IN AN
INDISTINCT CHECKERBOARD PATTERN REMINISCENT OF THE HOUSES OF NORMANDY. THE WALLS, EXCEPT THE SIDING
IN THE GABLES, ARE WHITEWASHED. THE EXTERIOR TRIM IS OF SOLID OAK, WEATHERED A DARK BROWN, AND
THE ROOF OF WOOD SHINGLES LAID IRREGULARLY, ALSO WEATHERED BROWN. THE LIVING ROOM, A CORNER OF
WHICH IS SHOWN ABOVE, HAS PLASTER WALLS, A MOTTLED WARM GRAY IN COLOR, AND OAK TRIM AND BEAMS IN
A NATURAL ANTIQUE FINISH. A SHORT FLIGHT OF STAIRS LEADS FROM THE LIVING ROOM TO A HALL, ON TO WHICH
OPEN TWO BEDROOMS AND A BATH AND FROM WHICH ANOTHER SHORT FLIGHT LEADS TO A BEDROOM AND BATH
OVER THE LIVING ROOM. THE BEDROOM AND STORAGE AT THE LEFT OF THIS HALL ARE STILL FIVE STEPS HIGHER,
SO THAT FROM THE LIVING ROOM TO THIS BEDROOM ARE FOUR DIFFERENT LEVELS

THE MAIN ENTRANCE OF THE KEFFER HOUSE, SHOWING THE COPPER HOOD OVER THE DOOR

THE HOUSE OF EARL EDWARD SANBORN, ESQ.

Ralph H. Hannaford, Architect

THIS HOUSE, LOCATED IN WELLESLEY, MASSACHUSETTS, IS OF WOOD-FRAME CONSTRUCTION WITH A VENEER OF HARVARD BRICK. THE LINTELS OVER DOOR AND WINDOWS ARE OF HEAVY OAK, AND THE ROUGH-CUT LAPPED BOARDS ON THE GABLE ENDS ARE OF WEATHERED CHESTNUT, GRAY IN COLOR. THE FENCE, DOOR, AND SASHES ARE PAINTED WHITE, AND THE ROOF IS OF DARK GRAY-GREEN SHINGLES. THE HOUSE HAS NO CELLAR, BUT A HEATER ROOM BUILT OF HOLLOW TILE IS PLACED TWO STEPS BELOW THE LEVEL OF THE FIRST FLOOR AND IS SEPARATED FROM THE MAIN PART OF THE HOUSE BY SELF-CLOSING FIRE-DOORS. THERE IS SPACE ON THE SECOND FLOOR FOR TWO ROOMS

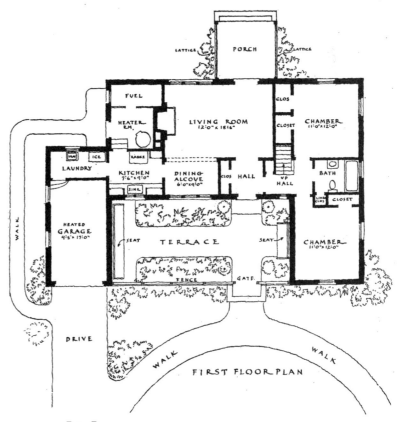

FIRST FLOOR PLAN

THE HOUSE OF FRANCIS E. FROTHINGHAM, ESQ.

Howe, Manning & Almy, Architects

OF WOOD-FRAME CONSTRUCTION WITH A VENEER OF WATERSTRUCK BRICK, THIS
HOUSE FACES NORTH ON A LOT IN CAMBRIDGE, MASSACHUSETTS. THE EXTERIOR TRIM,
FENCE, AND PORCH ARE PAINTED A CREAM COLOR AND THE ROOF IS OF UNFADING
GREEN SLATE. THE HOUSE HAS SATISFYING PROPORTIONS, SIMPLICITY, AND DIGNITY.
THE COLONIAL PORCH SHOWS EXCELLENT DETAIL

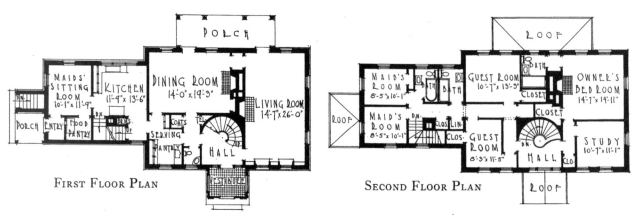

FIRST FLOOR PLAN   SECOND FLOOR PLAN

THE HALL HAS A DADO AND
WOODWORK OF WHITEWOOD,
PAINTED WHITE; THE WALLS
ARE COVERED WITH A FIG-
URED PAPER HAVING A GRAY
GROUND. THE STAIR WINDS
UP IN A PARTICULARLY
GRACEFUL CURVE

THE LIVING ROOM HAS PLAS-
TERED WALLS, COVERED
WITH CANVAS AND PAINTED
IVORY COLOR. THE MOULD-
ING AND PANELING OVER THE
FIREPLACE ARE ALSO IVORY
COLOR, AND THE FACING OF
THE OPENING IS COVERED
WITH BLACK CEMENT

THE HOUSE OF WILLIAM K. JACKSON, ESQ.

Henry Atherton Frost & Eleanor Raymond, Architects

THIS HOUSE IS BUILT ON A SLOPING LOT IN CHESTNUT HILL, MASSACHUSETTS, FACING
SOUTH. IT IS OF WOOD-FRAME CONSTRUCTION, WITH A VENEER OF SECONDHAND
BRICK WHICH ARE OF VARYING SHADES OF SOFT WARM RED, WITH ENOUGH OF THE
MORTAR LEFT ON TO GIVE THEM A BLOOM. ITS EXTERIOR TRIM, INCLUDING DOOR,
DOOR ENFRAMEMENT, AND BLINDS, IS PUTTY COLOR TO MATCH THE MORTAR, AND ITS
ROOF IS OF MOTTLED PURPLE AND GREEN SLATE

FIRST FLOOR PLAN

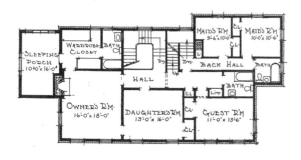

SECOND FLOOR PLAN

THE DOORWAY, OF BOLD
GEORGIAN DESIGN, IS THE
CHIEF DECORATIVE FEA-
TURE OF THE HOUSE. IT
IS LIGHTED BY A CON-
CEALED FIXTURE, BE-
HIND A GROUND-GLASS
PLATE SUNK FLUSH IN
THE OVERHEAD PANEL

A LOW HEDGE OF YEW
MARKS THE EDGE OF THE
GRASS TERRACE IN THE
FRONT OF THE HOUSE,
AND A HEDGE OF AR-
BORVITÆ ENCLOSES ONE
SIDE OF THE SMALL GAR-
DEN BY THE PORCH

[71]

THE SUNROOM AND SLEEPING PORCH AT THE WEST END OF THE JACKSON HOUSE HAVE MATCHED BOARDS ON THE
END AND WIDE CLAPBOARDS ON THE SIDES. THE WINDOW OVER THE DOOR SHOWS A BEAUTIFUL ADAPTATION OF
THE FAMILIAR PALLADIAN MOTIVE

The House of Fayette Baum, Esq.

Dwight James Baum, Architect

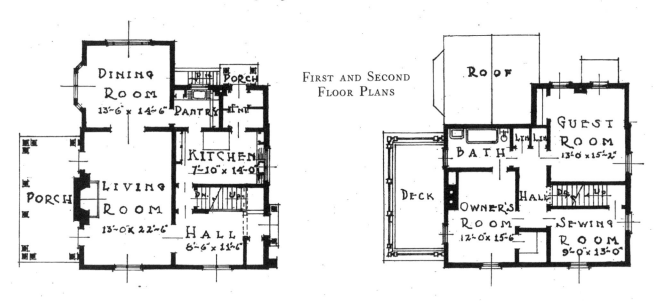

First and Second Floor Plans

THIS GEORGIAN COLONIAL HOUSE IN SYRACUSE, NEW YORK, IS BUILT WITH 8" BRICK
WALLS. THE EXTERIOR WOODWORK IS PAINTED WHITE, AND THE ROOF IS OF SLATE IN
GREEN, GRAY, BROWN, AND PURPLE SHADES. THE HOUSE IS SO PLACED ON THE LOT THAT
ITS ENTRANCE IS ON THE NORTH WITH THE LONG SIDE OF THE LIVING ROOM AND THE
DINING-ROOM BAY ON THE SOUTH

THE HOUSE OF LEONARD D. WHITE, ESQ.

Frank J. Forster, Architect

A HOUSE OF NORMAN ENGLISH TYPE AT GREAT NECK, LONG ISLAND

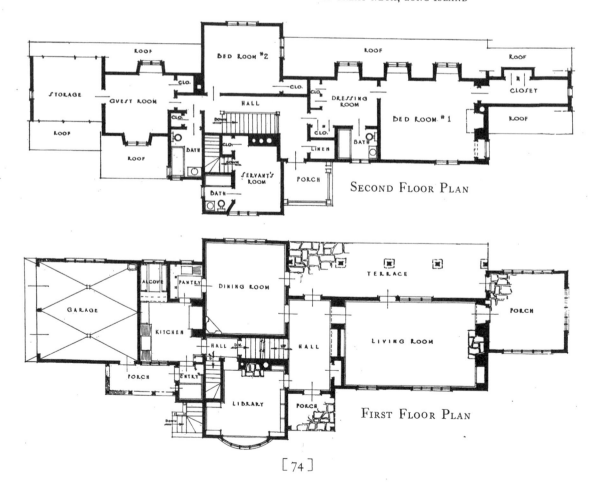

SECOND FLOOR PLAN

FIRST FLOOR PLAN

THE HOUSE IS OF WOOD-FRAME CON-
STRUCTION WITH A VENEER OF BRICKS,
WHITEWASHED, WHICH IN THE LIBRARY
GABLE ON THE FRONT ARE LAID TO MAKE
AN INDISTINCT DIAMOND PATTERN. THE
EXTERIOR WOOD IS ALL OF WEATHERED
OAK. THE ROOF IS OF UNEVEN SLATE
IN WEATHERED GREEN, GRAY, AND
BLUE TONES. THE HOUSE, 98' x 31'
OVER ALL, FACES WEST AND IS PLACED
ON A SLOPING LOT WHICH, AT THE REAR,
COMMANDS A VIEW OF LONG ISLAND SOUND

SUCH DETAILS AS THE LAYING OF THE
SLATE WITH A CERTAIN DEGREE OF
UNEVENNESS WHICH IS NOT TOO PRO-
NOUNCED, THE ROUNDING OF THE VAL-
LEYS WHERE GABLE OR DORMER MEETS
THE ROOF, THE SLIGHT CURVE OF THE
ROOF AT THE EAVES, MADE BY CORBELING
OUT THE BRICKS, AND THE CHARACTER OF
THE JOINTING OF THE BRACKETS WITH
THE POSTS WHICH SUPPORT THE PORCH
ROOF, ALL HELP TO GIVE THIS HOUSE
ITS CHARM AS MUCH AS DO ITS EXCEL-
LENT PROPORTIONS AND FINE WINDOW
SPACING

THE HOUSE OF WILBUR BRUNDAGE, ESQ.

Frank J. Forster, Architect

THIS HOUSE, 64' x 51' OVER ALL, OF THE NORMAN ENGLISH TYPE, IS SITUATED AT
DOUGLASTON, LONG ISLAND. IT IS OF WOOD-FRAME CONSTRUCTION AND BRICK VENEER,
WITH STUCCO AND HALF-TIMBER ON THE ENTRANCE PORCH AND GARAGE. THE WALLS
ARE WHITEWASHED AND THE EXTERIOR TRIM IS OF SOLID OAK, WEATHERED BROWN.
THE ROOF IS OF SLATE IN BLUES, GRAYS, AND WEATHERED GREENS

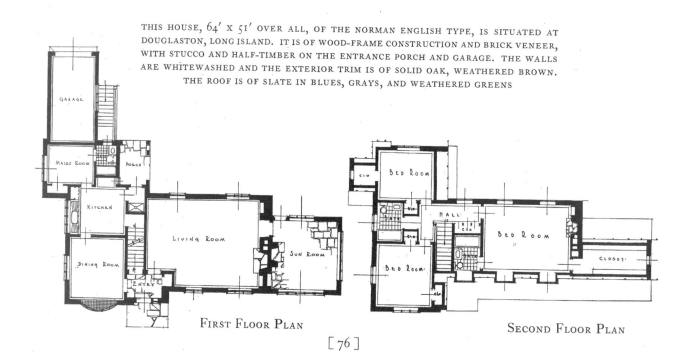

FIRST FLOOR PLAN

SECOND FLOOR PLAN

THE DETAIL OF THE MAIN ENTRANCE, AT THE RIGHT, GIVES A VERY GOOD IDEA OF HOW MUCH TEXTURE CONTRIBUTES TO THE ATTRACTIVENESS OF THE HOUSE. THE SLIGHT ROUGHNESS AND IRREGULARITY OF THE SLATE, THE USE OF SOLID OAK POSTS PINNED TOGETHER IN THE OLD MANNER, AND THE AVOIDANCE OF HARD, PRECISE LINES, ALL SHOW STUDIED ATTENTION TO SMALL MATTERS WHICH, IN THE SUM, MAKE ONE OF THE MOST IMPORTANT FACTORS IN DETERMINING THE ÆSTHETIC SUCCESS OF A HOUSE. THE PHOTOGRAPH BELOW SHOWS THE REAR OF THE HOUSE, WITH SERVICE ENTRANCE AND GARAGE AT THE RIGHT

THE HOUSE OF GERALD M. LAUCK, ESQ.

Frank J. Forster, Architect

BUILT IN MONTCLAIR, NEW JERSEY, THIS HOUSE, 47' X 48' OVER ALL, IS SITUATED
ON A SLOPING LOT WHICH FACES SOUTHEAST. IT HAS WALLS OF WOOD FRAME
WITH A BRICK AND STUCCO VENEER, WHITEWASHED. THE EXTERIOR WOOD IS SOLID
OAK, AND THE ROOF IS OF SLATE IN TONES OF BLUE, GRAY, AND WEATHERED GREEN

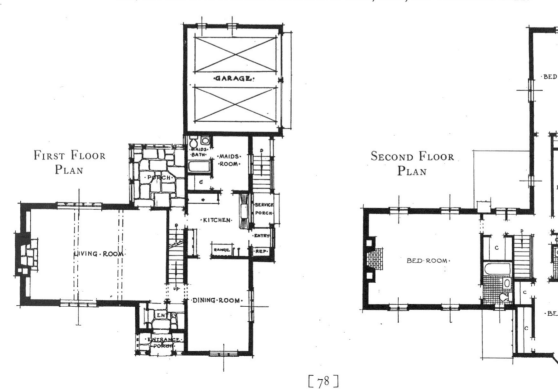

FIRST FLOOR PLAN

SECOND FLOOR PLAN

AT THE RIGHT IS A DETAIL OF THE
MAIN ENTRANCE, WHICH SHOWS
THE DELIGHTFUL TREATMENT OF
THE WOODWORK. THESE BEAMS
AND POSTS ARE MORTISED AND
TENONED AND ARE WEATHERED
BROWN IN COLOR

BELOW IS A VIEW OF THE FRONT
AND SIDE, WHICH SHOWS THE SERV-
ICE ENTRANCE AND GARAGE AT
THE REAR CORNER. THIS GARAGE,
ALTHOUGH LARGE ENOUGH FOR
TWO CARS, TAKES A PROPERLY
SUBORDINATE PLACE IN THE MASS-
ING OF THE HOUSE

THE HOUSE OF MORGAN BULKELEY, ESQ.

Philip L. Goodwin, Architect

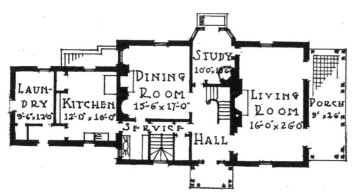

FIRST AND SECOND
FLOOR PLANS

THIS HOUSE, BUILT AT HARTFORD, CONNECTICUT,
FOLLOWS CLOSELY THE ENGLISH GEORGIAN
TYPE IN ITS GENERAL MASSING, ITS WINDOW
SPACING, ITS DETAIL, AND ITS USE OF THE BRICK
PARAPET CARRIED UP ABOVE THE CORNICE,
WHICH CONSISTS OF SLIGHTLY PROJECTING
MOULDINGS OF BRICK. THE HOUSE IS OF
WOOD-FRAME CONSTRUCTION, WITH A VENEER
OF COMMON BRICK; THE SHUTTERS ARE PAINTED
CREAM WHITE, AND THE HIP ROOF, WHICH IS AN
INCONSPICUOUS FEATURE OF THE HOUSE, IS OF
DARK GRAY SLATE

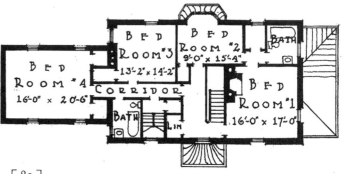

AT THE RIGHT IS A
DETAIL OF THE MAIN
ENTRANCE, WITH ITS
BEAUTIFULLY DE-
SIGNED LATTICE AND
WELL-TRAINED VINES.
THE DOOR IS PAINTED
GRAY-BLUE

BELOW IS A VIEW OF
THE REAR OF THE
HOUSE, WHICH OVER-
LOOKS THE GARDEN
AND RIVER BEYOND.
THE ATTRACTIVE LAT-
TICE AROUND THE
LAUNDRY YARD,
WHICH SHOWS AT THE
RIGHT, IS ALSO GRAY-
BLUE IN COLOR

THE HOUSE OF WILL HATCH, ESQ.

Dwight James Baum, Architect

THIS HOUSE IN CLEVELAND, OHIO, IS OF SOLID BRICK CONSTRUCTION. THE OUTSIDE
WOODWORK IS PAINTED WHITE, THE BLINDS ON THE SECOND STORY ARE GREEN, AND
THE ROOF IS OF DARK WOOD SHINGLES. THIS HOUSE WON THE THIRD PRIZE A SHORT
TIME AGO IN A COMPETITION FOR THE BEST DESIGNED HOUSE IN CLEVELAND OF ANY
SIZE OR COST

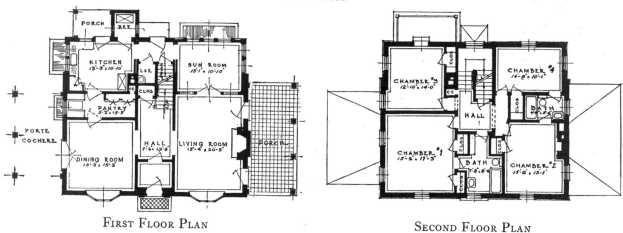

FIRST FLOOR PLAN   SECOND FLOOR PLAN

THE DISTINCTION OF THIS HOUSE IS DUE TO THE INTERESTING WALL TEXTURE GIVEN IT BY THE DEEPLY RAKED JOINTS, AS WELL AS TO THE REFINEMENT OF THE DETAIL OF THE DOORWAY, AND TO THE WINDOW TREATMENT

THE HOUSE OF KINGSBURY BROWN, ESQ.

Strickland, Blodget & Law, Architects

BUILT IN BROOKLINE, MASSACHUSETTS, THE DESIGN OF THIS HOUSE IS BASED ON THE
FAMOUS OLD DERBY HOUSE WHICH IS STILL STANDING IN SALEM. IT IS AN EXCELLENT
EXAMPLE OF A HOUSE HAVING DISTINCTION AND YET BEING PLACED WITH ITS FIRST
FLOOR WELL UP ABOVE THE GROUND LEVEL. IT IS OF WOOD-FRAME CONSTRUCTION,
WITH A VENEER OF HARVARD WATERSTRUCK BRICK; THE OUTSIDE WOODWORK IS
CREAM COLOR, AND THE ROOF IS OF BLACK SLATE. THE LOT ON WHICH THE HOUSE IS
PLACED FACES WEST, AND SLOPES ABRUPTLY UPWARD AT THE REAR

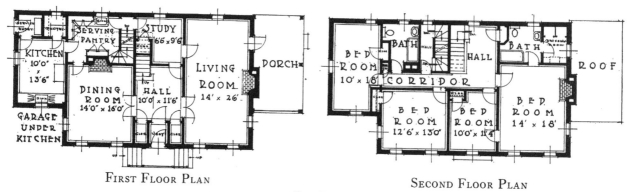

FIRST FLOOR PLAN

SECOND FLOOR PLAN

THE HALL SHOWN AT THE RIGHT
IS SHEATHED FROM FLOOR TO
CEILING IN CHESTNUT, IN WIDE
BOARDS OF RANDOM WIDTHS
WITH BEADED AND MOULDED
EDGES, AND STAINED WALNUT
COLOR. THE DINING ROOM,
SHOWN BELOW, HAS WALLS
COVERED WITH CRAFTEX OF A
PEARL-GRAY COLOR AND
SMOOTH TEXTURE, AND APPLIED
MOULDINGS OF THE SAME COLOR

A House in Houston, Texas

John F. Staub, Architect

OF WOOD-FRAME CONSTRUCTION WITH A
VENEER OF BRICK, WHITEWASHED, THIS
HOUSE WAS BUILT ON A LOT FACING SOUTH.
THE OUTSIDE WOODWORK IS WHITE, THE
BLINDS ARE DARK GREEN, AND THE ROOF IS
OF WOOD SHINGLES, ALSO DARK GREEN.
THE HOUSE HAS NO CELLAR, BUT THERE IS A
HEATER ROOM IN A WING ON THE LEFT

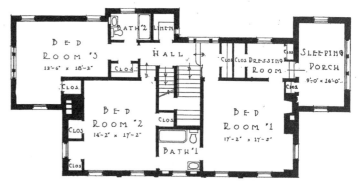

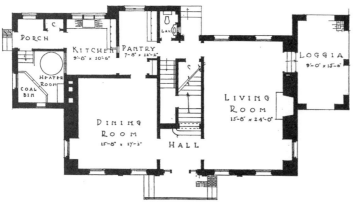

FIRST AND SECOND
FLOOR PLANS

[86]

THE IRONWORK, WHICH IS SUCH AN ATTRACTIVE FEATURE OF THE HOUSE, IS MADE UP OF OLD REMNANTS SALVAGED
FROM A JUNK DEALER IN NEW ORLEANS

THE HOUSE OF MACKAY STURGES, ESQ.

Aymar Embury II, Architect

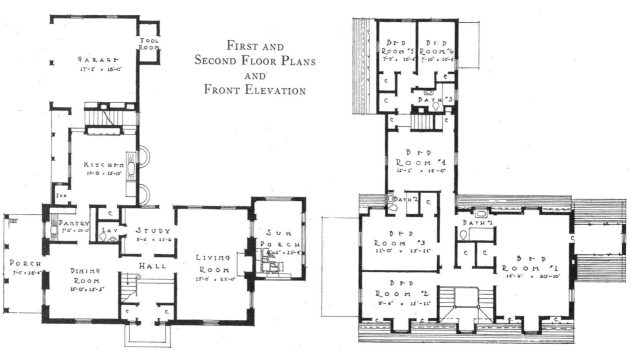

FIRST AND
SECOND FLOOR PLANS
AND
FRONT ELEVATION

THIS HOUSE OF DUTCH CO-
LONIAL TYPE IS LOCATED IN
PRINCETON, NEW JERSEY. IT
IS BUILT OF TERRA-COTTA
BLOCKS, STUCCOED IN THE
FRONT AND REAR, WITH ENDS
OF STONE TO THE EAVES AND
SHINGLES ABOVE. THE
HOUSE IS A FAINT GRAY, JUST
OFF THE WHITE IN COLOR,
WITH TRIM TO MATCH AND
WITH DARK GREEN SHUT-
TERS. THE ROOF OF WOOD
SHINGLES IS DARK GRAY. AT
THE RIGHT IS A DETAIL OF
THE FRONT ENTRANCE, AND
BELOW, THE LEFT END OF
THE HOUSE, SHOWING SERV-
ICE PORCH AND GARAGE

The House of Andrew Griffith, Esq.

C. A. Ziegler, Architect

WHAT MIGHT HAVE BEEN OUR FOREFATHERS' CONCEPTION OF A BUNGALOW, THE
ARCHITECT CALLS THIS HOUSE, WHICH HE DESIGNED FOR A CLIENT IN GERMANTOWN,
PENNSYLVANIA. IT IS BUILT OF LOCAL STONE, LAID WITH WIDE JOINTS AND WHITE-
WASHED. ITS OUTSIDE TRIM IS PAINTED WHITE AND ITS ROOF OF WOOD SHINGLES LEFT
TO WEATHER. THE HOUSE, 30' x 60' OVER ALL, FACES WEST

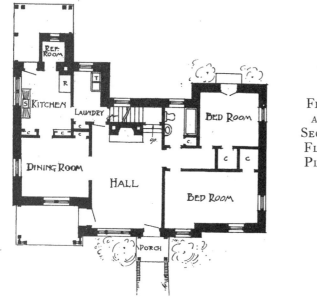

FIRST
AND
SECOND
FLOOR
PLANS

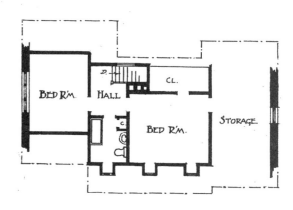

THE ENTRANCE SHOWS A BEAUTIFUL ADAPTATION OF THE DETAIL CHARACTERISTIC OF THE DISTRICT

THE HOUSE OF ROBERT T. MCCRACKEN, ESQ.

Mellor, Meigs & Howe, Architects

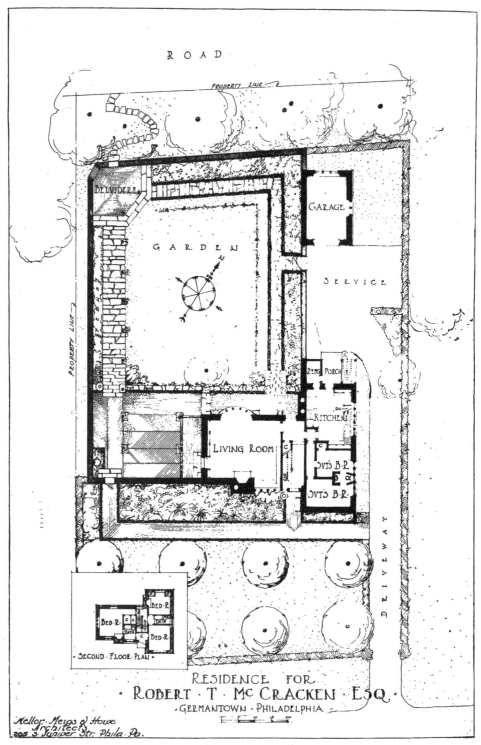

RESIDENCE FOR
· ROBERT · T · McCRACKEN · ESQ ·
· GERMANTOWN · PHILADELPHIA ·

Mellor · Meigs & Howe
Architects
205 S. Juniper Str. Phila. Pa.

THIS HOUSE IN GERMANTOWN, PENNSYLVANIA, IS BUILT OF LEDGE STONE WITH A
YELLOWISH GRAY TONE. ITS EXTERIOR TRIM IS DARK BROWN IN COLOR; ITS ROOF,
OF WOOD SHINGLES LEFT TO WEATHER. THE HOUSE IS 46' x 38' OVER ALL AND FACES
SOUTHEAST. THE PLOT PLAN ABOVE SHOWS THE DEVELOPMENT OF THE ENTIRE LOT, A
SERVICE THAT MANY ARCHITECTS CONSIDER AS IMPORTANT A PART OF THEIR WORK
AS THE PLANNING OF THE HOUSE ITSELF

A CORNER OF THE LIVING ROOM IS USED FOR DINING, AND CAN BE SHUT OFF FROM THE REST OF THE ROOM BY A CURTAIN. THE PANELED BENCH AND REFECTORY TABLE BESIDE THE TRIPLE CASEMENT WINDOW FORM AN ATTRACTIVE FEATURE AT ALL TIMES. THE WALLS OF THIS ROOM ARE OF SAND-FINISH PLASTER, BUFF IN COLOR, ITS WOODWORK OF YELLOW PINE, STAINED A DARK BROWN

THE FRONT OF THE HOUSE, SHOWING ENTRANCE DRIVE AND GARAGE IN THE REAR AND GARDEN AT THE LEFT

THE GARDEN SIDE OF THE McCRACKEN HOUSE, TAKEN FROM THE END OF THE GARDEN. AT THE LEFT A GAYLY
STRIPED GATE LEADS TO THE SERVICE COURT

THE HOUSE OF DEVEREAUX JOSEPHS, ESQ.

Robert R. McGoodwin, Architect

BUILT OF GRAY LEDGE STONE, OF ENGLISH COTTAGE TYPE, THIS HOUSE, 25′ X 95′ OVER
ALL, IS LOCATED IN CHESTNUT HILL, PENNSYLVANIA. IT HAS ITS MAIN ENTRANCE AS
WELL AS AN ENTRANCE TO SERVICE WING AND TO GARAGE ON THE STREET SIDE, WITH
LIVING ROOMS ON THE SOUTH, FACING THE GARDENS WHICH HAVE BEEN DESIGNED
ALSO BY THE ARCHITECT. THE CASEMENT SASHES ARE PAINTED A LIGHT GREEN; THE
ROOF IS OF VARIEGATED SLATE

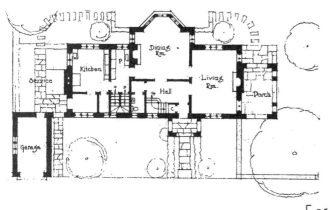

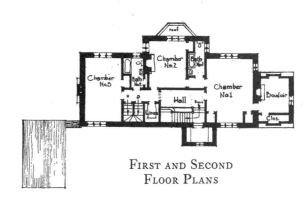

FIRST AND SECOND
FLOOR PLANS

The House of Albert Wilson, Esq.

Peabody, Wilson & Brown, Architects

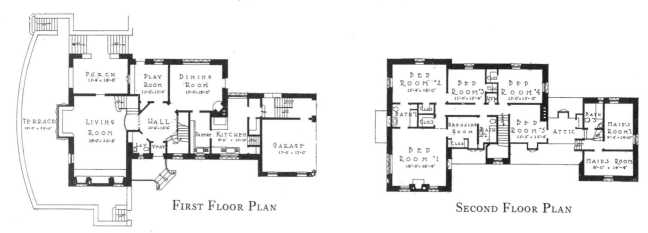

FIRST FLOOR PLAN

SECOND FLOOR PLAN

THIS HOUSE, WITH SOLID WALLS OF GRAY STONE, IS SITUATED ON A SLOPING LOT IN MAMARONECK, NEW YORK. THE UNEVENNESS OF THE LOT GAVE AN OPPORTUNITY FOR A CHANGE OF LEVEL ON THE FIRST FLOOR, AND THE LIVING ROOM, AS CAN BE SEEN BY THE PLAN, IS SEVERAL STEPS BELOW THE HALL. IT ALSO MADE POSSIBLE INTERESTING TERRACING OUTSIDE. THE HOUSE HAS STEEL CASEMENTS WITH SLATE SILLS, AND A ROOF OF BROWN SLATE IRREGULARLY LAID. THE DOOR IS OF NATURAL OAK

AT THE RIGHT IS A VIEW OF THE REAR OF THE HOUSE, SHOWING THE TRIPLE WINDOW IN THE DINING ROOM, AND A SMALL ARCHED DOORWAY WHICH GIVES ENTRANCE TO THE CHILDREN'S PLAYROOM

BELOW IS A VIEW OF THE MAIN STAIRWAY IN A CORNER OF THE OCTAGONAL HALL. THE WALLS IN THIS HALL ARE OF ROUGH PLASTER, YELLOW IN COLOR, AND THE WOODWORK IS ALL OAK WITH NATURAL FINISH

THE HOUSE OF MRS. CHARLES PLATT, 3RD.

Willing, Sims & Talbutt, Architects

A HOUSE OF PHILADELPHIA LEDGE STONE IN CHESTNUT HILL, PENNSYLVANIA

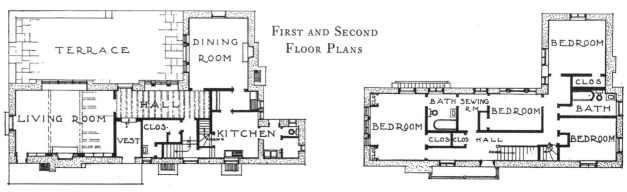

FIRST AND SECOND
FLOOR PLANS

THE EXTERIOR WALLS OF THIS HOUSE HAVE BEEN GIVEN A COAT OF WHITE-WASH, MIXED WITH A LITTLE YELLOW OCHRE. THE RATHER SEVERE FAÇADE ON THE STREET SIDE, WHICH IS BROKEN ONLY BY THE WOODEN BALCONY OF BEAUTI-FULLY TURNED BALUS-TERS AND THE STEPPED CHIMNEY, IS IN INTER-ESTING CONTRAST TO THE GARDEN SIDE, WHERE LARGE WINDOWS OF EX-CELLENT DESIGN OPEN ON THE PAVED TERRACE

AT THE LEFT IS A VIEW OF THE LIVING ROOM WITH A GLIMPSE OF THE HALL BEYOND, AND BE-LOW, A CORNER OF THE DINING ROOM. IN BOTH THESE ROOMS THE WALLS ARE OF PLASTER, PALE YELLOW OCHRE IN COLOR, AND THE WOODWORK, INCLUDING EVEN THE BEAMS IN THE LIVING-ROOM CEILING, IS OF THE SAME COLOR, GIVING AN EXCELLENT BACKGROUND FOR THE MAPLE FURNI-TURE AND BRIGHT CHINTZ

AT THE RIGHT IS A CORNER OF THE LIVING ROOM IN THE PLATT HOUSE, SHOWING THE GROUP OF FURNITURE AT THE LEFT OF THE FIRE-PLACE, AND BELOW, THE FIREPLACE IN THE SAME ROOM. BOTH THESE PHO-TOGRAPHS SHOW WITH WHAT SKILL PIECES OF FURNITURE OF DIFFER-ENT PERIODS BUT OF THE SAME CHARACTER HAVE BEEN ASSEMBLED AND WOVEN INTO THE SCHEME OF THE ROOM. THE PLAC-ING OF THE PIANO TO FORM A BACK TO THE COUCH OFFERS A VALU-ABLE SUGGESTION WITH REGARD TO THIS RATHER PERPLEXING PIECE OF FURNITURE